A Penny's Thoughts

Sometimes All You Need Is a Change of Perspective

TOMMY O'SIONNACH

Fulton Books, Inc.
Meadville, PA

Published by Fulton Books 2021

ISBN 978-1-64952-825-4 (paperback)
ISBN 978-1-64952-826-1 (digital)

Printed in the United States of America

For my parents, John and Jean—
thank you for the gift of faith.

Table of Contents

Acknowledgements

There are many people I would like to wholeheartedly thank for helping me cross this item off of my bucket list. I have always enjoyed writing and this experience has increased that love tenfold. I would have struggled mightily to complete it were it not for many fine people.

Thanks first and foremost to my parents, John and Jean for reading every word I attempted or actually put into this manuscript. The lack of curse words is most certainly a bi-product of their input! They are the best two human beings I know. I am grateful to my cousin Marty Fox, who like my parents has given feedback and support throughout. It should be known that the subtitle was 100% his idea. To my colleagues Steve Osewalt and Jim Krug for their grammar and punctuation help, I am truly grateful. I cannot neglect to mention all of my brothers and sisters who encouraged me to keep writing while the world was on lockdown. The six of you are the best friends a guy could ever ask for. I am forever in debt to author Kara Lawler who helped me across the finish line with this book. Every first time author should have a mentor as wonderful as her. Thanks to Chelsey at Fulton Books for answering all of my questions. If you are looking to self publish, Fulton Books is where it is at. Thanks to Lieutenant Colonel Raj Tuli for the amazing photography and helping create a mock-up edition of this book. Your friendship is a true blessing. To Justi, thanks for listening and showing me what a true teammate in life is. To Bridgie, Maggie, and Janey, the three of you are my world and the reason I strive to be the best possible version of myself every day.

Finally, I want to thank those folks that the characters in this book are either based or loosely based on. Whether on the shores of

Lake Erie or in the Laurel Highlands of Central Pennsylvania, my experiences with all of you inspired me to write this little book. I hope your stories bring as much joy to others as they have to me.

—Tommy O'Sionnach

Prologue

Growing up, I always wondered what certain inanimate objects would think if they had the same cognitive abilities as humans or animals. Of course, even as a kid, I knew this wasn't plausible, but that never stopped me from pondering this impossibility.

For one thing, many of the historical gaps we have would be filled if everyday objects or natural things could tell a story. The question of whether Leif Erikson or even Brendan the Navigator made it to North America hundreds of years before Christopher Columbus could be answered by rock formations where they first stepped ashore. A desk in the home of William Shakespeare could substantiate if the famous bard *did*, in fact, write all the amazing works he is credited with or if there was another person responsible. A tree in Dallas Dealey Plaza would clear up whether or not there was a second shooter involved in JFK's assassination. The list goes on and on. It leaves a lot to the imagination.

Of all the possible inanimate "storytellers" in America, the one that I believe would be most captivating has to be a penny or *one-cent piece*, as it is officially called. They are the well-traveled peasants of our monetary system and have bounced around for centuries, often with little or no regard from the citizens of this country.

In the same way, many of us have experienced what a penny goes through at one time or another in our own lives. Think about it: everyday people are overlooked, disregarded, seen as worthless, nonessential, and then, simply cast aside. As a result, we humans often find ourselves in search of meaning or on a quest to matter. Every person wants to mean something to somebody, whether it's to an employer, coworker, friend, neighbor, teammate, family member, or spouse. It is something that is ingrained in all of us, and a big part of our own feeling of self-worth. So who better to tell a story about the pursuit of significance and self-worth than the bottom of our financial totem pole? Told from the perspective of the currency that is most prolific yet incredibly underappreciated: the penny.

Mint Condition

Johnny Cash. What an amazing singer. So much of what he wrote beautifully summarizes the human condition. In fact, his lyrics describe all manner of existences, including mine. It's probably impossible to "be everywhere, man," but from where I am lying right now, I've probably come pretty damn close.

My family dates back to the early 1790s, so essentially we are about as old as this wonderful place called America. We have pretty much been the same shape and size and made of a handful of different materials. Some of us have bronze blood, some copper, tin, or zinc. Our looks have changed over the years, eleven times to be exact. Beginning as a lady with flowing hair, we've slowly evolved into our current look. From flying eagles to Indian heads, finally settling into the right-facing Abraham Lincoln in the early 20th century.

I made my illustrious entrance into the world on the 30th of September at 9:01:53 a.m. Myself and 1,039 siblings were born at that exact moment. A day of production usually yields 30 million of us. Funny thing is, these days, our kind costs more to produce than we are actually worth.

No person, animal, or coin, for that matter, should ever be made to feel worthless. The burning desire for significance is a fire that inhabits everything. I guess that's what makes it so tough for me and my brethren. Ours is inevitably an existence of rejection. Mother Mint has produced 288.7 billion of us in nearly two and a half centuries, and with 130 billion still living that crazy circulation life, the broad swath of humanity that has possessed us seems as numerous as the stars. An American tapestry is woven daily with the circulation of coins, and the fine print is written by the penny.

Vinny

One hundred of us were finally cracked and released into a register after what seemed like an eternity in that God-forsaken plastic sleeve. Having your face in one guy's butt and another smashed into yours is not a pleasant experience. Those fortunate enough to be first in the roll have it so good!

After seventeen openings and closings, I quickly deduced I was at a fast-food restaurant. Every time the till was opened, the pungent smell of deep-frying hash browns would fill the air. The hot cup of joe I made change for was bought by a man named Vinny. He was a short-stout fellow with a penchant for spilling coffee on his shirt. He was gregarious and spoke with a booming voice. From what I gathered, I was in the presence of a jack of all trades.

Vinny spent much of his career as a teacher, a proud achievement considering as a young man, he struggled with dyslexia. He worked for a limousine company part time as well, driving almost every celebrity imaginable. His favorites included George H. W. Bush and the band Chicago. He loved that they always invited him backstage to eat before the show. They were, as he would say, "A heck of a nice group of guys." An infamous British rock band was a whole different story. He often boasted of how he intentionally hit every pothole on a stretch of I-90 in order to disrupt their cocaine use to and from the show. The pile of *Daily Racing Forms* in the backseat of his champagne-colored station wagon revealed his passion for betting on horses, or his "other business" as he often said. But of all the different hats worn by Vinny, his coaching hat was his absolute favorite.

Vinny's perfect offense was basketball evolution at its finest. Like a maestro standing before his world-famous orchestra, the old coach would throw down five coins on any flat surface and begin to feverishly show how it could become the greatest offense ever devised!

I was honored to be one of those "players" during my time with Vinny. He really didn't differentiate when it came to what position I played; thus, I became familiar with all five spots on "the floor" with a salt or pepper shaker always serving as the basket. His masterpiece was based on five individuals that could play each position. All interchangeable parts. This was a revolutionary concept for many because the game has big and small, slow and fast, smart and well, uh, not so smart. It didn't matter. Vinny's offense was utopian in every sense of the word, but he believed it was possible, and Tommy would be the one to run it when *he* became a coach.

While on one of his many walks with his wife, Martha, Vin noticed that one of the Fox boys had really sprouted up. The gangly Tom had reached six feet five just prior to his eighth-grade year. Vinny had found his block of marble in which to sculpt his basketball "David." A player that could potentially do it all, regardless of his size, a concept that was ahead of its time when most players were typecasted to just one position. Thus began a truly unique friendship.

To say Vinny was an "out of the box" thinker was an understatement. When they started, he saw the opportunity to try all sorts of different techniques while training the very willing young player. Tommy was in love with the game of basketball, and as the fifth of seven children, he knew it could be his ticket to a free education and maybe more. Whether running around a track while dribbling a tennis ball or securing caroms as he worked with Vinny's one of a kind rebounding machine (a cross-like structure with a pulley and rope with a ball duct taped to the end of it), the creative coach's methods all had one thing in mind, to develop a ballplayer that would be able to play all five spots in his dream offense. Fortunately for Tom, there were no chasing chickens employed to improve his speed!

The handful of times I got to "suit up" for the coach truly were an honor and I hope helpful. I often wonder what Tommy would be thinking as Vinny choreographed different game-time situations. If he was confused, he never let on, he just silently nodded his head and asked questions when he could get a word in edgewise. I also recognized a sense of obligation in the young man, his attention and openness to learning were the least he could do for all the time and effort the old man had put into helping his dreams come true.

Life has a funny way of turning out though. While he hoped this interchangeable amoeba of an offense would transform the game, it was the unique methods of training that changed lives. Tommy and his two younger siblings, Peter and Mary, would receive full scholarships, and parents from all over the city began to request that Vinny work with their children, which, of course, he did; this saved families millions of dollars in college education.

Over the years, I have met other coins throughout the course of my travels that were used in a similar capacity by other coaches. I bet none of their "offenses" would stand a chance against Vinny's potential juggernaut.

And that is how I got to know the passionate, ever-devising, rotund little coach. He and I parted ways when he bought another coffee that assuredly was partially spilled on yet another shirt.

Barb

Undoubtedly, people often look at us as dirty and full of germs. And they have a point. I mean, it's not like we are polished by all those we come into contact with, as if part of some immaculate coin collection. Did you ever think that maybe it's the fault of our handlers that we are so unclean? Well, regardless, my shine had not yet diminished when I helped make change for a bottle of pop and a pack of cigarettes. Before catching a glimpse of my new owner, I was stuffed into a fanny pack that had a smokey, peppermint smell to it. From the sound of it, I was now the property of someone of the fairer sex, and she was in a bit of a hurry!

Barb was a slender middle-aged widow who stood about six feet tall. Her husband, Lou, was twenty-two when he died serving his country during the Tet Offensive in Vietnam. They hadn't been married a year when two officers appeared at her front door.

With no children to help cherish the memory of her heroic husband, Barb's life had become a very lonely one. When she wasn't working as a crossing guard for the kids at St. Luke's School, she could be found at the local Catholic War Vets Club smoking her cigarettes and playing the kind of games with pull-tab tickets. Barb never stayed at the club longer than a few hours because she could not miss seeing whom she called "the second love of her life," Alex Trebek, for her nightly episode of *Jeopardy*. This was routinely followed by a few episodes of *Matlock*, a bowl or two of rocky-road ice cream, and one last smoke before heading to bed. The next day would inevitably bring the same mundane routine that had made up the widow's solitary existence in the years since Lou's death.

Barb was normally a late riser. She had to be at her crosswalk by 6:45 a.m. and was always there right on time, which was a small miracle considering the time she woke up and the fact that she would stop every day at a local gas station for her soda and smokes. The process would have been much less stressful had Barb owned a vehicle, but she really couldn't afford one on what little she made, so it was never a priority. Of course, this didn't stop her from complaining about having to walk everywhere whenever she got the chance.

On the Friday prior to Veterans Day, Barb decided to indulge her affinity for low-risk gambling and bought a ten-dollar scratch-off ticket. The American lottery system has been around since our founding and helped bankroll this young nation; however, Barb had never won significant amounts whenever she played, with the most being fifty bucks. As she fumbled around in her fanny pack looking for a coin, none other than yours truly was chosen for the task! Now, it takes a deft hand to use a penny for a scratch off because unlike other coins, we do not have serrated edges. With vigor and enthusiasm, the two of us set out to reveal a winner, and three cherries later, Barb had won $5,000!

The next week, Barb decided she would use her winnings to purchase a car. The incredible selection of used vehicles at Mescan's Automart was probably her best bet. She was perusing what was in stock when a handsome gray-haired salesman approached. Her attention was immediately drawn to the Marine Corps insignia tattooed on his forearm. Turns out Paul was a Vietnam veteran and member of the Third Platoon with Lou all those years ago during Tet. He himself was widowed just a few years back after his wife, Debbie, lost her battle with breast cancer. They talked about everything but purchasing an automobile before he finally showed her what inventory he had to offer.

Now, I know my stay in Barb's fanny pack wasn't a very long one, but the woman that walked off the lot that day was not the same person that had arrived in search of a car. Gone for the first time in years was solitude and loneliness, replaced with a beautiful sense of hope. How else could you explain her decision to buy a *diet* cola? A purchase I gladly helped her make so she wouldn't have to break a twenty.

Owen

I often liken the opening of a cash register to the pulling of a slot machine. There is that old familiar *ka-ching* sound that echoes in our ears each time it happens. Humans associate that sound with coming into money, usually that money is the form of loose change being given after a purchase. When I first went into circulation, that sound was one of hope. Will I be selected? Who will I be joining? It was an exciting noise. But then, just like everything else, the novelty wore off. It became monotonous, tiresome, and at times, utterly annoying. Eventually, it became the anthem of the unknown. Our sort becomes indifferent to it rather quickly, especially during the holiday season when God knows how many freaking angels get their wings.

After sitting what felt like an eternity in that gas station's register, I was soon in the pocket of a little boy who could not have been more than ten. He had decided to use some of his hard-earned paper route money to buy a couple of packs of baseball cards and a blue slushy. Owen was a short red-haired kid with freckles who loved his card collection. He kept all those worthy of a *Beckett Monthly* rating safely inside one of his innumerable trading card sleeves. They were his pride and joy: a collection so meticulously cared for that it had become the envy of every boy living on Clifton Boulevard.

The two packs he bought yielded nothing new, besides of course two delicious powdery pieces of gum. Most of his haul that day would end up in one of his many shoe boxes filled with doubles and cards of players that didn't last long in the Major Leagues. Such irrelevance must be so humiliating. No sooner had that ginger put his collection away when I was suddenly plunged into the abyss.

Piggy-bank purgatory. Yep, you read that correctly. It's essentially our version of "the hole" you will find at state prisons across the country. The underbellies of those porcelain swine are dark, scary, and very uncomfortable. And let me tell you, those miscreant inmates have one luxury we do not, they get to be *alone*! The erratic infusion of more coins from that little slit in the ceiling is both violating and uncomfortably random. Like a wave in the ocean that unexpectedly pummels and de-pantses an unsuspecting vacationer. The anxiety associated with being "saved" is absolutely maddening. You wonder if this is how the rest of your days will be spent. Will I ever see the light of day again? And then, the bottom suddenly falls out, literally.

There is a transformation that occurs when that black rubber stopper is suddenly pulled out, and you fall out onto an unknown surface and see the light of day again. You go from the autonomous state of single currency to being a part of something much bigger. Not only do you get to see the faces of those you were sharing such a disconcerting limbo with for the first time, but you realize you were being saved for an important purchase. Something that will potentially bring a lifetime of joy to its owner, not just something insignificant like a candy bar. In our case, it was to buy a mint-conditioned 1992 Topps #768 Jim Thome rookie card. This treasure was not destined to be one of nine on a page sleeve. No. This card was headed for its own individual 3×4 top-loading hard plastic case. It was one of the finest purchases I was ever fortunate enough to be a part of, and the sparkle in the boy's eyes confirmed his happiness. Owen's parents had succeeded in teaching their child the old adage, "A penny saved is a penny earned." He savored it all the more because it was bought with *his* paper-route money. It was a microcosm of the American dream if there ever was one.

Thankfully, I wasn't long in that collectibles cash register before I helped make change for a hundred-dollar bill that was used to buy a vintage *Superman* comic book. My new owner was an awkward teenaged boy and would surprisingly be the human I spent the most time with during my circulation days.

Blake

Unfortunately, pennies are often seen as expendable. We have been lost in between couch cushions, placed on railroad tracks to be flattened, painfully elongated in some crank machine at a national park, or tossed into the dreaded little tray next to the cash register along with the other rejects to be used by some other patron that doesn't want to break a five-dollar bill. But sometimes our insignificance is given a glorious pause, most notably as the centerpiece of the iconic burgundy-colored penny loafer. A must for every preppy the world has ever produced, including my new owner, Blake.

I was quite fortunate on two counts. First, the tax on the comic book brought the total cost to $79.88, and second, it was the day before the start of school, leaving me and another fortunate chap as the only two candidates in Blake's pocket to be inserted into his brand-new loafers. Prior to being placed into the left laceless shoe, I was shined up, thanks to a luxurious vinegar-and-salt solution dip, followed by a thorough rinse under the faucet. I hadn't shown so brilliantly since the day I was minted, and up until that point in my life, I had never felt so important. Little did I know, the polish and my sense of significance wouldn't last long.

Daily life at Blake's all boys' prep school never disappointed. There always seemed to be something sinister being plotted by these hormone-raging, devious sons of privilege, and I had a daily front-row seat! The range of unruly behavior went from the innocuous—like duct taping a freshman to a tree in the quad—to the legendary release of a greased baby pig into the cafeteria. Regardless of the offense, the faculty of this prestigious Jesuit institution were always at the ready when it came to demanding one's JUG (Justice Under God) card, which would then result in an after-school detention.

It was a very physically taxing year on those poor loafers. Blake stood about five feet, four inches and weighed in at about two hundred pounds. He was a solid kid. Every morning, I would pray that Blake showered and put on clean socks before slipping into his shoes. If one, or God forbid, both of those things were not adhered to, I was in for a very unpleasantly pungent day.

As I mentioned, my newly acquired sparkle didn't last long. Like the *Shudras* of the Aryan caste system, shoes truly are the laborers of one's daily ensemble. Throughout that entire school year, I was exposed to seemingly every element of weather, with the absolute worst being the dreaded lake effect snow! For those unfamiliar with this wintertime nastiness, lake-effect snow is generated by cold air passing over warmer water and often produces a heavy and wet "heart attack" snow, which is a pain to shovel in the winter. Blake's house didn't have a garage, and since putting boots "would take too much time," I spent many a winter morning completely covered in that bitterly cold precipitation!

Life can be deceptive on many levels. So often we imagine certain existences to be ideal. Take Blake. He was the son of two doctors, drove a brand-new Jeep Grand Cherokee, had a spectacular comic book collection, and went yearly to a different "all-inclusive" vacation destination. Ideal life, right? Not in his eyes. He would have given anything to be a talented athlete or to be accepted by the "popular kids." Had he just counted his blessings he would have been much more content than he actually was? My time spent in his loafer taught me from the outside looking in, not everything is as great as it seems. Sure, longevity and being held onto for a purpose was a wish I had always had prior to my time with Blake, but nothing really matters unless you are thankful for whatever circumstances you are in. A grateful heart is a happy heart.

Life's little transitions come and go. For those of us in the currency world, they can be the difference between feast or famine. Of course, it all depends upon who you are with and where you are. I have been held on to for months, and I have been held on to for seconds. The one constant between passages has been time spent in a cash register, coin box, or some other sort of temporary holding cell.

So you can imagine the panic and terror that came over me when I found out Blake was planning to part ways with me by catapulting both of his loafers into a large dumpster.

He and his classmates were participating in the annual "loafer launch," a proud tradition dating back decades that marked the end of the school year. One by one, students would line up at various points surrounding an enormous dumpster and attempt to dispose of their school shoes, using all manner of homemade medieval weaponry. Blake and a few of his buddies had thrown together their version of a trebuchet. As they lugged it to their desired launching point, they were harassed by classmates for its pathetic appearance. I remember his friend Lyle yelling back self-deprecatingly, "This is a magnificent piece of garbage!" To look at it, you never would have thought it could have slung a marble, let alone a shoe, but that didn't stop his other friend Tim from proudly exclaiming, "It's a great day to be a physics geek!" As they counted down, I found myself wishing I had the ability to close my eyes, and the next thing I knew, I was suspended in midair before successfully landing in a foul-smelling waste monstrosity. I was panic-stricken. Was this how it was supposed to end for me? Headed to some god-forsaken landfill? I was both literally and figuratively plunged into the abyss, certain my days of circulation were over.

Edna

No sooner had the curtain come down on what appeared to be the final scene of Act II, ending my brief "performance" in circulation, when the most unlikely of people appeared, and plucked me from what I thought was to be my eternal perdition. Usually being rescued involves a "hero" of sorts I would suppose, but this person hardly fit the bill. In fact, she was the polar opposite of valorous.

Edna had lost everything a few years prior. Once the envy of every other housewife on Belle Avenue for her fashion sense and striking good looks, her marriage and family fell victim to the bottle. The drinking started out as something to help cope with the every-day stressors of middle-class America, but quickly degenerated into something she couldn't live without. Her husband, Fred, pleaded with her to stop for the sake of their children and for him. Attempts at sobriety were made, but they all ended in failure. Sometimes she was able to make it a few weeks, but then that familiar urge would set in. She would hide bottles all over the house from the linen closet to the cubby hole in the attic but would eventually be discovered, either by Fred or one of the kids. Finally, after a decade of self-inflicted debauchery, the family asked her to leave and only return when she had quit for good.

It didn't take long before Edna numbered one of the hundreds of homeless in the city. She was incapable of staying sober and, as a result, couldn't hold down a job; therefore, she could never make rent. Her "camp" was in the woods behind the football stadium. Everything she owned was inside an eight-by-eight-foot maroon nylon tent. Her new neighborhood was one of the larger areas where the less fortunate lived for a couple of reasons: first, because the own-ers of the football team kept port-o-potties open year-round in the parking lot; and secondly, it was close to many of the hunger centers throughout the city.

For the destitute, daily routines are essential for survival. Many of the basic amenities we take for granted can only be appreciated by the down and out. Showers are available at a handful of shelters and churches and, although not able to be accessed easily, provide a source of relief and dignity. In the same way, meals could be found once or twice a day, depending on how much Edna was willing to walk. She had also learned the best time to dumpster-dive at restaurants and grocery stores and knew the best time to pick out food that was still warm from the former. It's amazing how much perfectly edible food is thrown away on a daily basis.

Every Sunday, no matter how inclement the weather, a tall middle-aged man with a mustache would deliver dinner with some of his students. Edna looked forward to the conversation more than the food. She hadn't really understood loneliness until she started living on the streets. That teacher and his students became the highlight of her week for many months because she didn't really have many friends—well, besides Frank.

Frank was a fellow alcoholic that lived under a bridge near St. Malachi's. He was raised in an orphanage, never married, and had no children, at least that he knew of. Having roamed the city streets for most of his adult life. He was a professional vagabond, you might say. To look at him, you wouldn't guess he was homeless. Being probably in his late sixties and of average build, Frank kept his graying hair and beard neatly trimmed with a pair of clippers he had stolen from a drugstore downtown. Edna's relationship with the older man was platonic in nature; alcohol, of course, remained both of their "true loves" in life.

Frank took it upon himself to teach the "rookie" how to survive on the streets, and that is how she came to be pulling pennies out of worn-out loafers that warm evening in June. I spent numerous weeks logging countless miles in a drawstring Crown Royal pouch. It was what remained of the last bottle she took from her house on Belle and contained all the wealth she had accrued in her time since. The irony was not lost on me: in going from Blake to Edna, I had spanned the vast American income gap in the most unlikely of transactions.

That particular summer was extremely humid, and when you are a vagrant, there is really no escaping the elements. Frank's chronic asthma was beginning to take a toll on how creative he could be in finding daily meals. Oftentimes Edna, whose hair would become uncontrollably frizzy thanks to the sultry air, would stash food in her pockets from a free meal to bring back to him. While eating lunch at a food kitchen on the near west side, she overheard that over on East Thirty-Fifth, there was a little yellow house that provided fresh homegrown vegetables for the homeless. The house was owned by an older priest and middle-aged nun. Having at one time been a practicing Catholic, she thought this would be an easy way to get some produce and maybe enjoy the comfort of air-conditioning! So she set off on the two-mile trek, not realizing she was walking toward her saving grace.

Father Jim

Walking into the East Thirty-Fifth neighborhood was like entering a warzone. The once proud working-class neighborhood began to fall apart when the steel mills closed a decade before Gone was the modest paycheck to paycheck population, replaced with the down-and-out of society. It was here that a kindhearted priest and son of Irish immigrants decided to start his new ministry of hope.

As Edna entered through the front door, she was greeted immediately by a man who introduced himself as "Father Jim." He was probably in his late forties and looked the part of many first-generation Irish Americans on account of his fading red hair, fair skin, and blue eyes. His welcome was so genuine that Edna felt comfortable the moment she stepped into the house. After sitting down in a metal folding chair, she looked around the room at a most unexpected group of people. Gathered in that room were a few underprivileged people from the neighborhood: a married couple, a widow, a doctor that worked just down the road at a clinic, and about five or six octogenarian women from "the old country," whose spirited chattering filled the room with a lightheartedness that Edna hadn't felt in a long time. All of them were there as guests of Father Jim, no one more important than the other, ready to take part in a Mass.

Their celebration lacked the typical formality associated with Catholicism. Everybody was dressed very casually, and no one was expected to kneel, stand, or sit at required times. The lack of "Catholic calisthenics" created a beautiful simplicity that put Edna at ease. There wasn't even a collection before communion, but Edna was moved to give something for being made to feel so welcome, so reaching into her bag, she grabbed a handful of coins, me included, and placed us on a little table near her seat.

Father Jim was called to the priesthood from a very young age. He started his spiritual career as a parish priest and also served as the head of the city's CYO (Catholic Youth Organization), helping develop young parish athletes in grades four to eight. He was content with the capacity of work God had provided him until he was given an opportunity of a lifetime—a month to work side by side with Mother Theresa in the slums of Calcutta, India. The fire that this experience helped to light would burn strong and bright for all those he ministered to.

When he returned to American soil, Father Jim decided he wanted to help the poorest of the poor in his hometown. He set out in an old beat-up car and drove through some of the country's largest metropolitan areas, ministering to the homeless and helping to care for the sick. He lived among them in order to truly understand their plight. Finally, he realized his true purpose and, with permission of his local bishop, founded the Little Brothers and Sisters of the Eucharist, along with his dear friend Sister Maggie. Partnering with organizations like Habitat for Humanity, he began to rebuild the neighborhood and, with the help of many donations, bought the abandoned lots adjacent to his home and created one of the country's first effective hunger-fighting community gardens. From May through the end of September, neighbors would see him working while wearing his garden hat, lathered up in SPF 100 to avoid the sun's wrath on his pale Irish skin. His father taught him that such work was "like a prayer," and this particular "prayer" both fed and inspired many.

Because of his work, people from around the city began to care for their neighbors in ways they never had before. One gentleman, while cleaning out a closet at home, came across three letterman jackets once belonging to his sons. At that instant, inspiration struck. Why couldn't these coats be refurbished and given to the homeless? There were probably hundreds of old coats hanging in closets in towns all around. And so "Varsity Coats for Needy Folks" was born, bringing warmth to the downtrodden and a new purpose to these once proudly worn jackets.

The people Father Jim sought to help were of every age, race, gender, and creed. He did not discriminate. Edna's decision to search out food that muggy day would become her first step on the road to recovery. After her fourth Thursday night Mass, Father Jim convinced Edna to check herself into Rosary Hall, one of the first rehab facilities set up by the founder of Alcoholics Anonymous and run by the famed Angel of AA, Sister Mary Ignatia Gavin, who happened to be the good father's second cousin. Edna was overcome with a sense of hope and determination to *finally* get sober so she could reunite with her husband and children. As a sign of gratitude, she handed Father Jim her purple velvet bag, containing all the money she owned, and asked him to take it for his ministry. Welling up with tears, he said, "God bless you, Edna." It wasn't much but, like the widow's offering in the Gospel of Luke, meant more than any donation he had ever received. The next day, Sister Maggie gathered fifty of us into a paper roll and deposited us at a bank. Abandoned once again, I began to wonder if I would ever find a place to call home.

Penny Non Grata

I remember one time being in a woman's purse, her name escaping me, while she and her fiancé were at a pre-Cana meeting, a requirement for marriage in many churches. The speakers were talking about the various stages of married life. You know, from the honeymoon period, where everything is hunky-dory, to that period where reality sets in that this person, who always forgets to put the cap back on the toothpaste, is who you are stuck with for the rest of your life. They even referenced a period in all marriages known as the "desert." During this time, usually when children arrive, the bliss of the first few years of matrimony is a distant memory. In its place is a stark-new reality, and while we coins don't marry, I felt I had arrived at this dreaded place.

After being deposited that warm summer day by Sister Maggie, the best way I can describe the months that followed would be like some demented form of speed dating. I would venture that the most time I spent in someone's possession was two, maybe three days at most. It was a whirlwind where I was used in the purchases of everything imaginable. Too numerous to mention them all quite frankly. From pantyhose to snow cones and everything in between. The variety of inconsequential objects I helped purchase was staggering.

I am often needed when a person putting gas in their car can't pull off the "perfect pump" and even more notably as a means of saving various folks from having to break their beloved five-, ten-, twenty-, fifty-, or one-hundred-dollar bills. What was irritating was that the appreciation of my services was short-lived. The ultimate insult is when those one cent Canadian imposters are mistaken for one of us! I mean our dimensions are so different! The majority of pennies are resigned to the fact that this is how it is and there is no changing our insignificance. They respond with apathy. Not me. I just wanted to be appreciated. I wanted to mean something beyond my monetary value.

Those months were really starting to take a toll. At times, it felt like I was going through a moving hibernation, I was out there, but asleep, not registering where I was or who had me until the day a four-year-old girl found me next to their house and swallowed me in an attempt to impress her big sister. How I had ended up in their yard to begin with, I can't recall. That was the lowest point of my life. Looking back on it now, it's funny, but it was no laughing matter at the time.

Maggie was a middle child if there ever was one. Angelic one moment and devilish the next. When her father hoisted her and her sister Bridgid up to give them a first look at their baby sister, Jane, Maggie responded to her dad's question, "What do you think?" with "I don't know yet." Taking care of three little girls that particular summer had made it a hectic one for her father, a high school history teacher, and it hit a climax the day she swallowed me.

As I lay inside her little stomach with what appeared to be some chewed-up dinosaur fruit snacks and the contents of a juice box, I could hear the panic in her father's voice as he called the doctor. When he hung up, assured I would pass "unobstructed," a sense of calm overcame the beleaguered man. She would be okay. But what about me? Once again, I didn't seem to matter and was naively unaware of how vile the journey ahead of me was about to be.

There can't be too many experiences akin to being digested and pooped into a toilet bowl by a four-year-old. In fact, the day I plunged into that crystal-clear privy water, I felt how the astronauts aboard the Apollo 13 mission must have felt when they splashed down into the Indian Ocean on that historic April day. But instead of being rescued by a navy helicopter, I was plucked out of a piece of human waste by a much-relieved father. I immediately was cleaned off with soap and water, helping to enhance my new "stomach acid" shine and slipped into his pocket, safely out of the young girl's reach. Later that day, I helped pay for a six-pack of light beer, no doubt just the elixir that worn-out man needed. If he felt bad about using me for his purchase, he didn't show it. Can you imagine if that poor cashier had known where I was? My shock from the whole situation hadn't abated.

As I sat in a cash register for the 1,261st time since being minted, I decided to change my mindset. I *had* to believe people appreciate me more than not. That I wasn't as insignificant as it usually seemed. At least I hoped so. One thing that's for sure is hope makes life much more tolerable, so I clung to it in a way I never had before, ironically in the same way stink clings to s——t!

Val

America is an extremely fast-paced society that doesn't pause very often to catch its collective breath. People are constantly on the go and, regardless of how demanding, schedules are expected to be kept. It's a way of life we coins are all too familiar with. Money transactions occur day and night in every time zone from the Hawaiian Islands to the East Coast. The flow of currency between American citizens happens at breakneck speed. Whoever first coined (no pun intended) the phrase "stop and smell the roses" could not have been a citizen of the United States. So you can only imagine how rare it is to come across a person that brings peace to the madness of everyday life.

I was soon part of the change given to an older gentleman that had purchased a disposable camera. Val was a sixty-something retired engineer that spent over thirty years working at "Bell Telephone." He was a tall and slim former Marine that kept a meticulously trimmed beard and was rumored to use the same pair of scissors to edge his freshly cut grass.

The grip of his handshake, soothing voice, and complete attention he gave to those with whom he spoke affected people in two ways. First, it lowered that individual's blood pressure for some reason. He had an incredible knack of putting people at ease. Some people need medicine for their hypertension, but had they known Val, it would not have been necessary. A ten-minute conversation with him would do the trick. Second, he made you feel important. That is an amazing gift to have. While conversing with him, besides the calming effect he had on each individual, the undivided attention he gave every person, no matter who they were, seemed to transcend a normal, everyday conversation. In fact, talking to people and getting to know their story fascinated Val. He once decided to take a four-day bus trip home after flying one of his daughters to the west coast, where she was beginning a new job. To most, that sounds like a horrific experience. For Val, it was an enjoyable opportunity to talk with new and interesting people, something he did throughout the forty-seven-hour bus ride in between naps.

I had not spent large amounts of time with retirees before Val. His days were spent in ways I never would have expected. Most Americans have an idyllic view of retirement that includes relaxation and a huge reduction in work. It appeared at first that I was now in the company of such a retiree. He had bought the camera to capture shots of wildlife as he made his way down river. It was a picturesque late summer day. I had never been on the water before, and I loved the sensation.

As we glided along in his green kayak, Val would occasion-ally anchor along the bank, crack an ice-cold beer, and wait for his Pulitzer Prize moment. But this wasn't the norm for him. He was an indefatigable artisan and a tireless laborer. His day started early and rarely ended before supper, usually being prepared by his wife of many years, Mary. This can certainly be attributed to his upbringing in a small coal-mining town, where the lazy would never survive, and was reinforced during his time in the service. I wouldn't be sur-prised if his picture would be found right beneath the words "former marine," *if* they ever existed in the dictionary, because there is no such thing as a "former" marine in this country. Once you serve in that proud branch of the military, you never leave.

Val's "retiree" days were spent cutting grass on a local farm, helping a number of not-so-handy young husbands fix various things around their respective houses, trapping all manner of vermin that had been terrorizing the neighborhood, tinkering in his garage on one of his many projects, and if time permitted, heading up to his favorite watering hole "Mike's" for a few glasses of beer and conver-sation with his pals John, Denny, and Fred. Inevitably, Val would spend most of his time at the bar listening, and when he spoke, it was always about what his kids and grandkids were up to. I have to say that in what is quickly becoming a "cult of me" society, being with someone that didn't want the spotlight was special. On cue,

Val would look at his old wristwatch, finish his last gulp of beer, and tell the boys he had to be home for supper. After dinner, he could usually be found sitting with Mary on their old cedar back porch swing, listening to the creek run behind their house and watching the assortment of wildlife come and go as the sun set on another day of "retirement."

In my quest to matter, Val taught me that significance doesn't have to be accompanied with heaps of praise, awards, or even press clippings. Importance and meaning are defined by being there for people. Whether it was by creating a one-of-a-kind sitting bench out of various wooden planks in his garage for a depressed friend, helping to catch an elusive skunk that was tormenting a neighbor's dog, or simply listening to something most would consider unimportant, Val's intention was never praise. It wasn't about recognition or "Atta, boys!" It was about being *present* for those he cared for or even hardly knew, and no one did it better.

I parted ways with Val on a golf course. He and Mary were playing the back nine of a local golf course when he used me to mark a ball he had hit onto the green. After lining up his putt, he flicked me aside, then proceeded to sink a fifteen-foot putt to save par. Unfortunately, in the course of his celebration, he forgot to pick me up. As he put the flag back and walked off, I was sad to see him go, but felt happy for those lucky enough to cross his path in the future.

Leroy

There are various superstitions and old wives' tales associated with discovering and picking up a lost penny. Many ancient civilizations believed that metals were gifts from their gods. From the Lydians onward, discovering a stray coin was considered a sign of good fortune for the finder. Of course, I don't know how those ancient deities would view those of us made of zinc. I would suspect that once they understood the metabolic properties of zinc and its importance to a healthy immune system, we would have been just as important as the silvers and coppers of the world.

I had spent the night on that beautifully manicured green, treated to a clear night under the stars, but once again unsure of where I was heading next. While admiring a beautiful sunrise over the eighteenth hole, I was suddenly scooped up by an elderly groundskeeper named Leroy. As he put me in the pocket of his overalls, I heard him mumbling to himself, "Find a penny, pick it up, then all day you'll have good luck."

Leroy had an uncanny resemblance to the great advocate of emancipation, Frederick Douglass. His wildly unkempt hair was partially bridled by a faded green bandana, and he was always wearing his old grey dungarees, mended in various spots with a variety of colorful patches. Some say he was the only groundskeeper to work the eighteen-hole gem, which was designed by a little known local semi-pro named Carl back in the early '50s.

One never knew what kind of mood old Leroy would be in on any given day. At times, he would shout congratulations if he saw a really incredible shot; other times, he would be cursing out someone that didn't pick up their divot or forgot to rake out a bunker. No matter how much he offended the player on the receiving end of his ire, the groundskeeper was never fired for his actions. He may have been given a slap on the wrist by the club pro or one of the starters, but even that was rare because no one kept a course as immaculate as Leroy.

Leroy referred to the eighty-eight-acre course as his "Mona Lisa." He would often greet golfers with a warning of, "Y'all be good to Miss Mona today." For those that didn't know him, it had to be confusing! But he was sincere in his words. Leroy saw himself as an artist, and those grounds were *his* masterpiece. Behind the bristly facade was a man that knew every aspect of USPGA (United States Professional Golf Association) standards. From the required green lengths before and after Memorial Day to the proper aeration techniques needed in order to loosen up soil that became too compacted, you would have never known Leroy only finished the ninth grade. What he lacked in formal education, he made up for in pride and knowledge of his craft.

I've noticed that this sort of craftsmanship doesn't really exist as it once did in everyday occupations. More and more, the modern workforce seems distracted by all manner of things. Maybe it's all the new gadgets that have been invented to make jobs easier or the increased desire for instant gratification in the younger generation of workers. Whatever it is, the Leroys of the world are sadly becoming fewer and fewer, and that worries me. Places like Parkwood Golf Course have become synonymous with the people that pour their blood, sweat, and tears into them and may one day cease to exist when the work goes from something to be proud of to something that's done for a paycheck.

Leroy always ended his workday with the same routine. After cleaning the equipment, he would stop by the kitchen and grab a hot dog with extra mustard, a bag of chips, and lemonade and then go sit on a bench behind the clubhouse that overlooked the ninth green. He loved watching golfers struggle against the hole's deep bunkers and his pin placement for the day. As he entered the kitchen, he noticed that a new girl, no more than twenty-one or twenty-two, was behind the counter. She seemed nervous as the old man approached. Before she could say anything, he said, "Welcome to Parkwood.

Folks around here call me Leroy." After ordering his standard meal, Leroy grabbed me out of his pocket and handed me over to the new employee. "Maybe this here penny will bring you luck in getting some good tips from these rich folks. Found it this mornin'." Then grabbing his meal, he headed for the door, leaving me with the daunting task of bringing this complete stranger good luck.

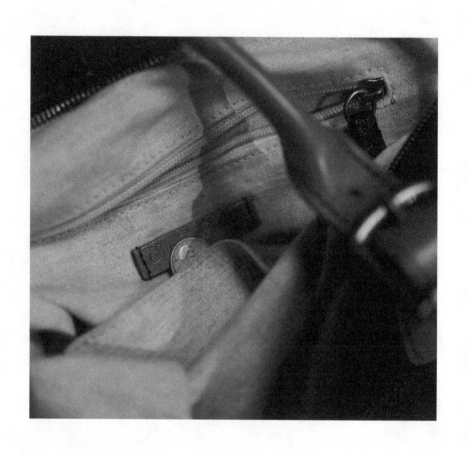

Whitney

Luck was never Whitney's forte. It seemed to avoid the young lady like winning seasons evade Cleveland sports fans. While it was a nice gesture on behalf of the old groundskeeper, she doubted it would lead to anything. As Leroy walked out the door, she tossed me into a rather pathetic-looking tip jar that had accumulated very little signs of customer appreciation at that point. Seeing as golf is a game for the wealthier members of society, you'd think her old mason jar would be overflowing with monetary kindnesses, right? Nope. This just reinforced my belief that just because you have a lot of money, doesn't mean you always share it.

Whitney grew up without any siblings. Her childhood was spent like most members of Generation X, outside. Summers were for riding bikes and playing with neighborhood kids until the streetlights came on, not spent in front of a screen. In what would be the final years before gaming systems started to hypnotize America's youth, the outdoors provided the ultimate sense of freedom.

Whitney felt most comfortable in nature with her "friends," the birds. Her father helped stoke her passion for ornithology when she was very young. The two of them had a small identification book that was published in the 1940s, and with it, they identified dozens of different species. They spent hours every summer in the woods behind her grandparents' house hoping to find some of the rare birds listed so they could put a checkmark next to its name or picture. Her childhood had been a happy one, that is, until Flight 83.

She vividly remembers the last time she saw them as they backed out of her grandparents' driveway en route to the airport. Her parents were going away to celebrate ten years of marriage over the long Labor Day weekend. The tiny prop plane went down in a dense fog seven miles off the coast of Nantucket, and all on board were lost, causing the lives of many, including nine-year-old Whitney, to be changed forever. The once joyful and confident girl may as well have been on that plane too. In her place was a reticent child who buried her grief by self-quarantining most days in her new room at her grandparents' house. The trajectory of her life was redirected in a way that would form her into the person she was the day Leroy gave me as a good-luck gift.

Whitney was about as indistinct of a young woman that has ever owned me. If you came across her in the street, you might have thought she was a secretary or maybe a librarian. Her sandy-brown hair was always up in a bun or ponytail, and her glasses were so thick that if you held them up to the sun, you'd be able to burn a hole through cement. She was seen as very quiet and bookish to all who *even* noticed her in high school. The sadness that saturated every fiber of her being the day her parents died had never left. She was raised by her paternal grandparents and, because of this and her insatiable appetite for reading, developed into a rather "old soul." Her grandma and grandpa loved her but were also dealing with their own grief. Whitney was a constant reminder of the son they had tragically lost, and they were just not equipped with the ability to nurture their orphaned granddaughter the way her parents would have.

The position at Parkwood's kitchen was one in a long line of post-high school employment. Her typical days since graduating consisted of going to work, reading, and usually ending on the old moss-covered log that she and her dad used to sit on while watching for birds those many summers ago. No doubt battling depression and apathy about the present and the future, the monotony of her everyday life had become the accepted routine. I guess I just couldn't understand how anyone could live that way. But countless people do. Gone are aspirations or the desire to live their best lives. In its place is an old familiar complacency that becomes harder to break with every day that passes. Whitney, still engulfed in unspeakable grief all those years later, was well on her way to making this the norm—well, that is, until I showed up.

About five minutes before the end of her shift, Whitney took the pathetically filled tip jar and dumped it into her rather cavernous purse. I had been inside numerous female accessories by this time and was surprised that a girl in her early twenties would be toting around a handbag worthy of an AARP member. Women's purses are truly a cornucopia of the unknown. Most females have a pocketbook for cash and change, but every now and again, usually when someone is in a hurry, you get thrown in with the general contents population. Among the usual items like makeup, gum, and tissues, Whitney had her treasured bird book, a small pair of binoculars, and a tiny camera.

Twenty minutes later, the view changed from an outdated kitchen to one of natural beauty in a wooded area that overlooked a man-made lake. The serene spot was located on her grandparents' property and was easily her favorite place to be on earth. It was here where she spent the happiest days of her life with her dad classifying birds, fishing, and catching lightning bugs. It was here where she fled when she heard about the demise of her parents and everyone on board that doomed flight. And it was here where she spent countless hours as a young adult. It was as though she was going through life just treading water, hoping not to drown. Fear arrived on that bleak September day when she was nine and had never left.

The mossy log was an ideal seat for birdwatching. From waterfowl to woodpeckers, the area was a perfect habitat for all sorts of different birds. Whitney could still hear her father's voice describing each of the beautiful winged creatures as she watched them. On that particular day, a strikingly handsome cardinal was busy helping his mate design a nest in the hollow of an immense oak tree. There is a peace that you feel when watching this process, and just as with humans, the female seems to be in charge!

The cardinal was her favorite for a couple of reasons: First, because they represent hope, health, joy, and rejuvenation—things that seemed to be significantly lacking in Whitney's life. Secondly, because of the belief that cardinals appear when deceased loved ones are near, and it is their way of sending their love. As she rummaged through her purse in search of her disposable camera, the sun shone like a spotlight directly on me and the words "In God We Trust." At that moment, Whitney could hear her father's voice as an indescribable peace came over her. It was as though he was saying, *It's time to start living again*. Fear and sadness were replaced by optimism and a new sense of purpose. It was a spiritual encounter unlike any she had ever experienced before. Her father had made his love felt by sending a beautiful red-winged messenger to pull his daughter out of the darkness as only he could.

I remained in that big paisley-covered purse for the rest of the week and halfway through the next. It's amazing how a change in one's countenance affects the amount of tips they receive. The smile on Whitney's face seemed to make club members much more generous. Her indifference to a well-organized purse enabled me to ascertain that all the other gratuities, and I would be spent on a nicer camera as soon as she had enough money. She wanted to buy a good one for the photography course she had just signed up for at the local community college. As the department store cashier handed her the receipt of her purchase after unceremoniously dumping me and some other change into the register, he asked, "Do you have any spots in mind to try out this new Kodak?" Nodding, Whitney remarked, "Pretty sure I can think of one."

Bobby

When you are stuck in a register, there are not many ways to entertain yourself. You hope that it won't be long, but sometimes, it unfortunately is. Recently, a new way of paying has become very popular. It's called a charge or something to that effect. All I know is when a customer says, "I'll just put that on my card," the drawer stays closed. So that can't be good for us, right? Anyway, I eventually was given as change for a big and tall polo that was on supersale. The guy who bought the shirt was a heck of a large man that could have passed for a starting left tackle in the National Football League. When he got into his pickup truck, he emptied me and some others into a cupholder, adding to what I would soon discover was his iced tea slush fund. For a week or so, I idly lay there, annoyingly stuck to another coin.

Bobby had always been big. He entered the world at fourteen pounds, twelve ounces, shattering the hospital record by over a pound. His name was given to him by his grieving mother and father a few days after Robert F. Kennedy died from an assassin's bullet. The Polish immigrants had defected from their homeland to escape the brutality of Communist rule. They came with the clothes on their backs and a devout Catholic faith that had been suppressed for years. As many who emigrated here, they were inspired by the essay Robert's F. Kennedy's brother John had written, referring to America as *a nation of immigrants*. Like millions, they mourned when he was gunned down in Dallas, but the pain they felt after Bobby's death was much more profound, and so after a grueling twelve-hour labor, they welcomed his namesake into the world.

Bobby's mother, Maja, was thought to be barren, so the forty-five-year-old and her husband believed her pregnancy was a gift from God. She referred to Bobby as *moj cud* or "my miracle." Just as miraculous is how they kept food in the house while Bobby was growing up. Raised on traditional Polish cuisine like perogies, kielbasi, and haluski, the sight of Bobby eating at the table was as much of a fixture in their home as the framed picture of Pope John Paul II that hung in their foyer.

By the time he entered high school, Bobby was a solid 6'5" and 240 pounds with meat hooks for hands. He was persuaded to go out for football, but it didn't take. He didn't like hitting people for fear he would hurt them—a true gentle giant. Instead of football, Bobby's passion was working as a volunteer paramedic. The feeling that came from helping people gave him deep satisfaction and would lead to his job in organ transportation for transplant procedures.

During his first few weeks on the job, while training under the woman he was preparing to replace, Bobby asked every question that crossed his mind regarding his new career. He wanted to make sure that when he took over, there would be no surprises. But just as in life, nothing can prepare you for everything. No amount of the future retiree's tutelage could prepare him for a career of "spanning the bridge" of emotions on a daily basis. Living in one of the top ten biggest metropolitan cities in the country kept the massive man busy traveling from hospital to hospital, delivering the lifesaving organs he was entrusted with.

You might think a job such as Bobby's would be fairly easy. Go get a cooler from one hospital, drive it to another, drop it off, and repeat. What many don't realize is the 180-degree swing in emotions that occurs when you "span the bridge" from pickup to delivery, or rather, from grief to joy. Most people that perform the same job as Bobby usually don't ask what happened to the donor. But Bobby always inquired and, depending on who was working, usually got an answer. Maybe it was the fact he was a volunteer paramedic or that his mother always encouraged him to pray for whoever had tragically passed away, but Bobby wanted to know who the hero was that was about to save the person awaiting his delivery.

A few days after I joined the rabble of coins in his truck, Bobby was on the scene of a car accident with members of his town's volunteer fire department. The victim was a college sophomore that he recognized from his church, St. Casimir's. In fact, he remembered being at the boy's First Holy Communion years back. His condition was critical, and thankfully, full-time paramedics arrived about the same time to attend to the twenty-year-old who was driving home for Christmas break. As the ambulance tore off, Bobby said a quick prayer for the young man and headed for home.

It was the Tuesday following the accident when Bobby's beeper went off. He was planning on attending the company holiday party, but there was a thirty-five-year-old in need of a heart. Bobby made his way to Sacred Heart hospital to pick up the newly harvested organ for transport. As he was signing off for the precious cargo, he overheard one nurse mention to another how Christmas will forever be ruined for that poor college student's family. Immediately, Bobby's own heart sank. No, not him. Pulling his hat down to hide the tears in his eyes, he made his way to his truck, and when he shut the door, he began to sob uncontrollably. After composing himself a few moments later, he took a deep breath and started up his truck, wondering if he could hold it together after he had "spanned the bridge."

The sadness Bobby normally felt for a donor and his or her family was always genuine. He wondered what kind of life he or she lived and hoped that they had at least experienced happiness before their lives were cut short. But this was different because he knew the boy that this heart originally belonged to. He had his whole life in front of him! *Why do things like this happen*? His anguish began to overflow moments after completing the delivery. *I can't even remember his name*, he thought as he walked away.

A few minutes later, Bobby was sitting in the hospital chapel, continuing to grapple with his emotions and the anger he was starting to feel toward God for taking such a young life. No sooner had the thought left his head when he was startled by a mother with a baby on her hip shushing three other young children as they entered the chapel. After they slid into a pew a few rows in front of where he was sitting, Bobby overheard the oldest of the children ask, "Why did we come in here, Mommy?" She responded, "We need to ask God to keep Daddy safe while he gets his new heart." The man whose mother called him her miracle suddenly realized that he was truly a part of one, not only that day but every time he clocked in.

As he drove home, Bobby remembered his mother had asked him to grab some sour cream for the Kolacky cookies she was planning to make, a holiday tradition. Doubling back, he made his way to the store, still trying to process the day's events.

Upon arriving, he noticed an elderly woman ringing her bell next to a big kettle. Before he got out, he scooped those of us, both stuck and unstuck, out of his cup holder and deposited us into the red pot and wished her a Merry Christmas. Peace on earth was something out of his control. Thankfully, the "goodwill toward men" part was something he was reminded of every day he went to work.

The Bullet

The freefall into that giant red kettle was both good and bad. Good, because I was finally separated from the coin I was stuck to. Bad, because I would spend the next twelve days in a frigid holding tank having to listen to that incessant bell for what seemed like an eternity. I have to say I admire the older woman who spent her holiday trying to get donations. As a coin, you feel good that you were used to help others, but it just stinks that none of us ever get to see how. From what I understand, that generous group of people really makes a difference all over the world. So after those twelve days, which were not nearly as fun as the song makes them out to be—I never saw a partridge or a freaking pear tree—it was time to be counted.

The world was introduced to the expression "variety is the spice of life" when William Cowper published his poem "The Task" in 1785. This is true on many levels with the exception of counting coins. When it comes to that, variety is a pain in the butt. Quarters, dimes, nickels, and pennies all vary in diameter, thickness, and weight and for years had to be rolled by hand into those not-so-flashy paper sleeves. I'm sure most Americans, at some point in their lives, have participated in this dreadful activity. But modern technology is a wonderful thing, always making time consuming tasks easier; and with the introduction of coin counting machines, yet another aspect of life was made easier.

Although I think I would prefer the old-fashioned way, it was definitely exciting when they dumped us down a shoot that led to all these sensor lights, rotating discs, and automated detectors, which eventually funneled us into a paper-sleeve-lined cup. For a second there, I could have sworn I heard "Night Fever" by the Bee Gees. Once fifty pennies were in place, the sleeve was sealed and then

dropped into the appropriate pile. The whole process was very dis-
orienting. When it was finished, I was taken to yet another bank and
then distributed to a hospital cafeteria. I was in the middle of being
volleyed back and forth between there and the hospital's gift shop
when I was pocketed by a policeman who had just bought a deck of
playing cards for a patient.

As he made his way down the corridor, I could hear the sound
of laughter coming from the room at the end of the hall. Inside were
three young nurses surrounding the bed of the man responsible for
their amusement. They seemed more like giddy teenage girls at a
Backstreet Boys concert than medical professionals. Looking up, he
saw that his friend Fitzy, the police officer that I was in temporary
residence with, had arrived and wished the attractive young nurses a
pleasant weekend as their shift was about to end.

The man laid up was a fireman named Jack who had survived
one of his department's worst tragedies. A propane tanker that had
been in for repairs at a local garage exploded while he and a few
companies were on the scene working to contain a leak. The deadly
blast that had killed four other brave men, including one from his
firehouse, launched Jack across a four-lane highway, slamming him
down awkwardly against a cement curb. The accident, combined
with the early onset of Marie-Strumpell spondylitis (a form of degen-
erative spinal arthritis), had made the thirty-something fireman very
familiar with hospitals due to the numerous surgeries he required.

Fitzy was a childhood friend who walked the beat around St.
John's Hospital. Most days, he came during his lunch break, but
before leaving the day prior, Jack had asked him to show up at about
2:45 p.m. instead of noon if he could make it work, adding that
it was extremely important. The bedridden fireman also gave him
five bucks and asked him to buy a deck of cards so he could teach a
very attractive young nurse that worked second trick how to play gin
rummy, claiming it would improve his prospects with her once he
got out of the hospital. As Fitzy pulled up a chair, he handed Jack the
cards along with his change. He hastily put us into a bedpan beside
his bed and motioned for his visitor to move in closer. Behind the

curtain that separated the room was a man snoring loudly, almost obnoxiously, and it was clear that something had to be done.

Speaking in a very hushed tone, Jack whispered, "Okay, Fitz, here's what's going to happen." Pointing at his holster, he continued, "You are going to hand me your gun and then walk out into the hallway for five seconds. When you hit five, come back in, take your piece, and get the heck outta here." The lifelong bachelor had clearly hit his breaking point. "This knucklehead snores all the freaking time and since they moved him in here yesterday morning. I haven't slept a wink."

Fitzy responded, "Have you finally lost it?" But he could see his friend was both serious and desperate, so against his better judgement, he handed him his nine millimeter but, before letting go of it, reminded him, "Just because we call you 'Bullet' doesn't mean you can fire one at anybody."

From the time he could walk, Jack found his way into all sorts of precarious situations. It was believed that he bought his first carton of cigarettes with his First Communion money and used the little that was left to begin a lucrative gambling enterprise. His nickname *Bullet* was given to him as the result of a time he was being chased by his father after he discovered his fifth-grade son was running dice games and taking bets all throughout the neighborhood. Determined to give the boy a taste of his leather belt, the old man gave chase as Jack darted through a series of garbage cans with scary precision. His father couldn't replicate a sharp cut the young boy had made and fell ass over teakettle after tripping over the last trash bin. Jack, who claims to have patented the "hummingbird start," hovered over his father, still moving in place. When he saw he was okay, he took off like a "bullet," not to be seen for a few days.

After graduating high school in the principal's office for one too many pranks, his parents thought the military would help straighten their son out. He did this two years, got out, then after spending a short time as a pipefitter, found his calling as a member of the fire department. It was a job that brought out the best in Jack. He distinguished himself as a damned good fireman and quickly earned his way up to captain. In one instance, he saved a woman from a collapsed building, and as soon as he pulled her from the inferno, she went into labor, and he delivered a healthy baby boy.

It probably wouldn't be a stretch to say that the Bullet wasn't the type of individual that could be entirely straightened out. He worked hard and, at times played just as hard. He spent his free time pursuing beautiful women, playing cards with his buddies, and betting on the ponies. A few times, he was reprimanded for taking bets on the firehouse phone, and he once got away with bringing a past love interest on a fire run. He loved to drink, smoke, and sing. He got away with things that most people never could, and I had a front-row seat for one of his greatest exploits.

As soon as Fitzy had left the room, Jack pulled back the divider that separated him from his snoring neighbor. After startling him and with the gun pointed directly at the man, he calmly said, "I swear to God, Andy, if you snore again, I'm gonna blow your head off!" He then quickly pulled the curtain back, handed the weapon to his friend, who disappeared down the hall without being noticed because of the shift change, and began to feign sleep. The Bullet had made sure all bases were covered in the execution of his devious plan as any good gambler would.

Fitzy could hear screaming from the first floor as he exited the building. Shaking his head at yet another one of his friend's ridiculous stunts, he hoped the police wouldn't be called in on this matter of which he had dubiously played a significant part. Then it hit him that *he* would get the call! Talk about a full-circle plot!

Meanwhile, Andy was in full-blown panic. As the evening-shift nurses arrived, he was screaming, "He's got a gun!" over and over.

Acting as though he had just woken up and with a confused look on his face, Jack said, "What are you talking about?" He then added, "You sure it wasn't a dream?"

Andy, clearly in shock at what had just transpired, demanded they search Jack's bed, to which he acquiesced. Finding nothing, Andy continued to rave on about the gun. Clearly not satisfied with the efforts to find the weapon, he was sure he had seen, Andy demanded he be moved to another room. Problem solved. With the snoring gone, Jack slept like a rock that night, convinced the ends definitely justified the means.

I remained in that bedpan for a few days until it was time for Jack to be released from the hospital, a process that always seems to take longer than it should. Walking out, he kissed each one of the nurses on duty and slipped his number to the attractive young brunette he had intentionally lost to while playing cards over the last few evenings, hoping to reap the rewards of his sandbagging.

A buddy from the firehouse picked him up, and the two went to take advantage of happy-hour prices at their favorite watering hole. In the course of their conversation, his friend, whose name was Marty, asked him whom he liked in the Derby. Jack, who never liked to bet on the big races, told him he didn't have a preference; besides, he had to be back to work at the Engine 14 house that day. "What if I were to tell you that I had two seats in the grandstand courtesy of my father-in-law?" Marty asked.

"I'd tell you it's too late to get a replacement to work my shift tomorrow, but I still think I should join you."

The rest of the evening, he went back and forth trying to decide what he should do. How often does a guy get the opportunity to see the Run for the Roses at Churchill Downs?

The next day while taking his lunch break, Jack called his friend from a phone behind the bar at a place near the firehouse, hoping he hadn't left for Louisville yet. After the second ring, he picked up. "Hey, Marty, it's Jack, glad I got you before you left." Then reaching into his pocket, he pulled me out. "So here's the deal, I'm gonna flip this coin. Heads I go with you and tails I go back to work." Placing me on his thumb, the Bullet flicked upward; and after rotating over and over, I landed on the bar, heads up. "Good news, Marty. It seems as though God wants me in Kentucky. Come pick me up in ten minutes behind Rungy's Place." And with that, he put out his cigarette and headed for the backdoor, leaving me on the bar with a few dollars' tip.

Joanie and Luis

I felt conflicted. What had just happened? One second, I am in this guy's pocket; and the next, I'm in midair flipping over and over. Did I really just determine a decision based on how I landed? Who does that? Then it hit me: I had just experienced my first coin toss.

Coin tosses can be viewed in two ways. Some believe it is putting fate in the driver's seat for an important choice that someone must make while others see them as instruments of divine decision-making. Personally, I just see them as either random luck for the winner or misfortune for the loser, both of whom are too scared to make a decision for themselves.

History has seen some famous coin tosses that have determined fame, fortune, and sadly, death. One thing that's for sure is no one knows the success of calling heads or tails right away. Think about it. When Richie Valens won a coin toss for the last seat on a plane that fateful day "the music died," it was a double-edged sword. Tragically, the young rock 'n' roll star lost his life; but because of the result, years later, that sad story would bring wealth to a lot of people who made a movie about it. In 1903, Wilbur Wright bested his brother, Orville, in a coin flip to see who would get the first crack at flight on that famous stretch of beach in Kitty Hawk, North Carolina. But his victory was short-lived when he was unable to capitalize on it by getting their plane in the air. Three days later, Orville recorded the first successful flight. That coin-toss victory meant nothing. As for me, I just hoped how I landed wouldn't cause any harm or bad luck for that fun-loving fireman.

I was soon on the move again. I ended up as part of the change for a takeout order of chicken wings. The man who bought the food then proceeded to a local grocery store to pick up some other necessities. I assumed he was headed to a party based on the things he had purchased. With a young daughter in tow, he kept promising to get her a gumball on the way out if she behaved. After checking out, he reached in his pocket and pulled me out and handed me over to his daughter, who couldn't have been more than five or six. She placed me in the slot and was turning the handle a smidge to the right when I got stuck. She had mistakenly inserted me in a gumball machine that was for dimes, not pennies! I was lodged so that only half of my face was showing. The child then began to cry because she didn't get her stupid gumball, and her father responded by giving her a quarter and having her pick another machine, completely ignoring my state of distress! They left me stranded there, and numerous people similarly just walked right by, doing nothing! Finally, my Good Samaritan showed up and dislodged me. The assistant manager that thankfully came to my rescue was a wiry blonde named Joanie. As she was locking the front doors of the store, I somehow caught her attention; and after yanking me out, I was then dropped into a decorative beer stein on her desk.

Joanie must have been in her late twenties, and judging from the picture on her desk, she was happily married with two sons. But just as with so many of the people I have come across, everything wasn't as perfect as it seemed. Her husband, Luis, was a caregiver at a local nursing home; and from what I overheard of their phone conversations in the office, the two of them had been drifting apart since the birth of their second child. They worked opposite shifts in order to avoid paying day care, and while it saved them financially, it wasn't helping their marriage. The few times they did see each other during the week were basically spent taking care of things around their three-bedroom house or running places with the kids. Instead of human beings, they had become "human doings" and, in the process, lost their connection to one another.

As I began to settle into my new surroundings in the office next to the produce section, an unexplainable anxiety seemed to descend upon the store. In what I had thought could only have been explained by an impending snowstorm, there was a mad rush on many items with the most sought after being toilet paper. After the fifth day in a row of similar shopping patterns, it became apparent to me this wasn't the doing of old man winter; rather, it was something much more serious. Soon store patrons were required to wear masks before entering, and the managers placed tape all over the store to enforce something called "social distancing." The grocer even created special hours for older people. All of these actions became a new sort of normal.

Luis was a broad-shouldered former swimmer when he and Joanie met in college. The two of them were in a freshman psychology class together and started out as friends before eventually dating and ultimately professing their vows. A classic case of opposites attract with him being an extrovert and she an introvert, they had always made a fantastic team, but selfishness had clearly corroded their once well-grounded relationship. They began to think more as two *me*s rather than one *we*. Part of this was also because of where they worked. Luis's job provided him with very little satisfaction. Yes, as head of activities at the Fir Avenue Nursing Home, he was beloved. He brought enjoyment and fun to the elderly on a daily basis, but calling daily bingo to a group that was collectively hard of hearing just wasn't doing it for him. Similarly, spending time taking what seemed like an endless amount of product inventory, coupled with the dreaded cleanup on aisle 9, was hardly fulfilling for Joanie. The pandemic changed this for both of them.

As the world seemed to sink into a widening chasm of despair, the perception of the word *hero* began to change. America has seen her share of catastrophes, and it's during these times that the important contributions of everyday workers come into focus, more so than those who normally get the limelight. To their credit, many musicians, professional athletes, and celebrities were some of the first to say thank-you to those people on the front lines battling the virus day in and day out. Joanie and Luis both bravely did their part, although in completely different ways.

Oddly, work at the Ravenna Street Grocer seemed to shadow Beethoven's Fifth Symphony. Much like the timeless classic, there was a cyclical frenzy that seemed to rise and fall throughout the workday. The crazy thing is, there was no real pattern to the insanity with so many people holed up at home. Grocery stores are obviously essential businesses needed for survival, and they *had* to stay open, so Joanie's role as assistant manager took on significant meaning for society. Inventory turned from the monotonous to the essential. The conjecturing of the media induced panic in millions of citizens, and supermarkets became ground zero for surly consumers intent on stockpiling sanitation wipes. A few times Joanie had to step in between angry soccer moms intent on wiping down the world as they both reached for the last container.

People want to feel that they matter in the big scheme of things, and after years of working a job that was taken for granted, Joanie found new pride in her work. Too often it seems to take unfortunate events or situations for people to receive their well-deserved praise and adulation, but I suspect that most of those underappreciated people never sought notoriety to begin with. The desire to be a valued employee is caused by the inevitable drudgery that all new jobs eventually evolve into, and sadly, it takes something catastrophic to make them feel appreciated again.

Luis's experience at work changed as well. Whereas Joanie's importance was rooted in helping to keep people fed while at the same time exposing her to hundreds of shoppers a day that *could* be contagious, Luis's most important role came in being with those that *did* have the virus. No amount of schooling could have prepared the former sociology major for the role he would have to play for dozens of dying residents.

Popularity comes with a price. A big part of Luis's job was to bring joy to those in the twilight of life, and the success he was able to attain in doing so made him the obvious choice of both his superiors, and the families unable to be with their loved ones, to be there during their final moments. Luis's tender blue eyes seemed to be amplified when he wore his surgical mask. They were the last thing many residents saw before closing their own eyes for the last time.

He was witness to how this virus maliciously attacked the elderly. One day, a resident was fine, and the next they were on death's doorstep. His employer made sure he was properly attired with medical supplies before entering rooms, but as for his supply of emotional strength, that was another thing.

I would guess many people try not to think about death, especially of a loved one. Therefore, I would also suppose that most people don't put much thought into being there with that person in the moments before they die. The pandemic changed that. The majority of the world showed compassion by sheltering in place, but if a member of their family was about to die at the hands of the sinister virus, they were locked out from being a part of those final moments. They couldn't say goodbye in person. The families of the Fir Avenue Nursing Home had become all too familiar with this; but as painful as it was, they were comforted to know Luis would be there, holding his phone closely so that husbands and wives, brothers and sisters, children and grandchildren could say their tearful farewells. Each time he had to do this, he was filled with a variety of emotions, ranging from deep sadness to profound gratitude. Often, he would receive a call days after someone had passed, or a card thanking him for risking his own health so that they could have that final moment.

Those dark times really began to reshape life inside Joanie and Luis's modest split-level home at 4311 Lakewood Avenue. Everything became more meaningful, especially the few moments they got to see each other in between shifts. Things that had become the same old boring routine, like taking a family walk or sitting on the couch watching a movie, were cherished with a zest like never before. With so many things shut down, life seemed to grind to a beautiful halt. It was as if God hit a reset button and gave them a better understanding of what was truly important. This was the silver lining of the havoc that COVID-19 had wreaked.

As the resilience of the American people began to win the war against the coronavirus, life began to return to normal. Things inevitably sped up, schedules started to return, and the myriad of everyday distractions became available once again.

After locking up the store on a beautiful June evening, Joanie came back to the office, grabbed me out of the beer stein, and exited through the loading dock out back. I could hear the unmistakable sound of crickets as she walked toward what I assumed was home.

Before I knew it, she was standing before a beautifully lit-up fountain in the center of town. Not a soul was around. As the soft spray of the fount caught a warm summer wind, she began to speak. "The last few months have brought terrible suffering to so many. But at the same time, it healed what was broken in my marriage, and that's crazy when I think about it." Then pulling me out of her pocket she said, "My wish is that Luis and I don't lose each other again." With that, she flung me into a beautiful three-tiered marble fountain, and it seemed my time in circulation had ended as a wish.

Patrick

Fountain—to a penny, the word is synonymous with heaven. The age-old tradition of throwing coins into these beautiful water-infused structures has most certainly been experienced by much of humanity at one time or another. Whether it's one being tossed into a fountain at a shopping mall or three being thrown into the world-famous Trevi Fountain in Rome, there is an ambiance of hope that comes as a result of this simple tradition, and I am thrilled to now be a part of it. Being the proxy of a heartfelt wish, well, I don't know if it gets any better than this. Dozens of wishes are made every day by both young and old, and I'm sure the sight of us glistening in this crystal-clear water is probably a very beautiful vision indeed.

I have been spending my days mostly thinking about the past. About the places, things, and most importantly, the people I have come across. I would guess they numbered well into the thousands, and there is no way I could recall every stop on my journey, but I wonder how things turned out for those that were in possession of me at one time or another.

Whenever someone's time on earth comes to an end, the people that knew and loved them, unless they lived to a ripe old age, probably see their lives as an incomplete jigsaw puzzle. There are pieces missing; it is not finished yet. There are gaps and empty spots that should have been filled. I am sure Barb and Whitney could relate, having lost those closest to them at such an early age. Bobby's job makes him all too familiar with the tragic loss of life as well. For him, it must seem like that organ he delivers goes from a lost puzzle piece to one people rejoice over finally finding. If people would just look at the beauty of what was completed instead of focusing on the empty spaces, my guess is they would go through life happier.

People are like pieces themselves when I think about it. Some are like those flat-edge border ones that everyone puts together first. They create structure and provide you with a vision out of the chaos of the pile, much like Vinny did for his players or Father Jim did for society's downtrodden. Some pieces seem to be lost due to their nondescript appearance, and you have no idea where to put them, much like Edna and so many others we number among the poor in this country. Or kind of like how Blake must have felt when he was labeled a NARP (Non-Athletic Regular Person) by one of the popular jocks that one time in gym class. At times, I felt that way myself, being a penny and all. Then there are those coveted transition pieces that help to make the connection between two different sections of the puzzle, much like Val was able to do with people. Other pieces are searched for diligently, and when they are found, they provide a satisfaction that Owen must have felt when he added to his hard-earned baseball card collection or that Leroy experienced when he looked out across that picturesque par-three he diligently made sure never lost its difficulty or appeal.

The last few stops on my journey to this fountain, built in honor of a hometown soldier named Patrick who was killed when he fell on a grenade in combat, helped me to understand a line from a prayer that I heard every day while in Blake's loafer. In the "prayer for generosity," I was initially struck by the words "to give and not count the cost." I scoffed when I first heard those words because I considered myself an expert when it comes to the purchasing process, and it seemed silly that someone would just hand over money. But then one day, I started to realize I had it all wrong. The lines that follow in that prayer, made up by some guy named Ignacio, go on to say:

> To fight and not heed the wounds,
> To toil and not to seek for rest,
> To labor and not to ask for reward.

These were things I learned in my brief time with Jack, Luis, and Joanie. The fact that Jack was in that hospital for months due to his bravery was not something I really thought about or the fact that a pandemic would bring out the best in Luis, Joanie, and countless others. Those words rang truest in how the three of them reacted because they didn't count the cost, seek rest, or ask for any reward. They embodied the true spirit of those words, just as the namesake of this fountain did a few years prior in Iraq.

Speaking of Patrick, I recently found out that the coins tossed into this fountain never stay here forever, something I thought was standard procedure for all of us wishes. The Trevi Fountain in Rome supposedly brings in around three to four thousand euros a day, and the money is used to feed the poor of the city. Likewise, though obviously to a lesser extent, every year, the money thrown into Patrick's memorial fountain is taken out and put toward a college fund for his two young daughters. So it appears as though I will soon be on the move again, and I can't wait to see who I'll be blessed to be with next.

For now, though, I am content just living in the present moment. Had this been my mindset during all the twists and turns of my journey, it certainly would have quelled many of the fears and anxieties I felt weighted down with along the way. But hindsight is *definitely* twenty-twenty, and wherever I go from here, instead of focusing on the belief I have been relegated to some unsavory place, I intend to relish the fact that somebody found the need to keep a penny.

About the Author

 Tommy O'Sionnach is a native of Lakewood, Ohio, who currently resides in Altoona, Pennsylvania. For the last twenty years, he has worked as a social studies teacher at the high school level. A former Division I college basketball player, he also established Ultimate Bigman LLC and has run camps in Pennsylvania, Ohio, New Jersey, and Ireland. He is a father of three daughters: Bridgid, Margaret, and Jane.